sixty more sermon illustrations

david adam

kevin mayhew

First published in 2007 by

KEVIN MAYHEW LTD
Buxhall, Stowmarket, Suffolk, IP14 3BW
E-mail: info@kevinmayhewltd.com
Web: www.kevinmayhew.com

Sixty More Sermon Illustrations is extracted from *Searchlights*, Complete Resource Book, Year C.

9 8 7 6 5 4 3 2 1 0

ISBN 978 1 84417 718 9
Catalogue No 1500969

Cover design by Sara-Jane Came
Edited by Katherine Laidler
Typesetting by Katherine Laidler

Printed in Great Britain

Contents

Signs of glory

New life in Christ

The life of faith

Introduction

This second book of sermon illustrations was compiled with the busy minister, preacher or speaker in mind: it can be a daunting task to find a fresh theme or topic each week and these short pieces will hopefully be a handy resource. They are meant to help provide that sometimes elusive topic or to amplify an existing central theme.

Visual aids often speak more directly than words and these short, vivid illustrations, as well as illustrations from your locality, can help you to throw light on the Scripture passages and to relate them to what is happening in your community or the world.

By referring to the two indexes (Topical and Bible reference) you can decide how to plan the sermon or expand on your own theme. The cross-referencing means that you have quite a few ideas at your fingertips.

1 God waiting and watching

Aim

To show how God delights in all who turn to him.

Readings

Luke 15:1-10

Illustration

A letter from God

When you awoke, I was there, waiting upon you. I wanted to share in your love.

At breakfast you listened to the radio and rushed your breakfast. You had no time to speak to me. I waited but you did not turn to me.

Though you travelled by rail you spent your time on your laptop and reading the news. You did not once give me a thought. And I waited for you to turn to me.

During your work there were lots of small gaps. There was more time at lunch. But you did other things and had no time for me. Yet I waited for you to turn to me.

At the end of the day you watched the television and played a game. For a while you dozed before you had your last drink of the day. And I waited for you to turn to me.

Now, I thought, you will have time – just before you go to sleep. Instead, you read until you were tired. You worried about tomorrow and at last fell asleep.

I will surround you with my love this night. I will wait for you tomorrow and if you do not remember I will be there the day after. I will wait until you turn to me.

All my love, God.

2 Letting God in

Aim

To encourage people to trust in God and to invite him into their daily life.

Readings

Luke 12:32-40

Illustration

Look at Holman Hunt's painting 'Light of the World'. Here Christ is at a door knocking. The lack of a handle on the outside of the door shows it can only be opened from within. The weeds around the door show that it has not been opened for a long time. The apples lying on the ground remind us of the fall from grace in the Garden of Eden. Through sin, people and God become separate. Jesus comes to unite us again with God if we will let him into our lives.

3 The peace of Christ's presence

Aim

To show that Christ offers us his peace and his presence.

Readings

John 14:23-29

Illustration

In the old days crossing the Atlantic in a sailing boat left everyone to the mercy of the wind and waves. How those old wooden boats rocked about! People not used to the rolling of the boat could not walk on deck. Many had to spend most of their voyage below deck. Everything that could be was fastened firmly down to prevent it from being washed overboard. Today's journeys are a great contrast. Waiters can carry soup and children can play on deck. People lounge in the sun and hardly notice the rising and falling of the waves. Even in a storm the main body of the ship remains relatively calm – all because of the unseen gyroscope that maintains the balance of the ship. We have been offered the power of peace and calm in our lives through the presence of Christ. Do we accept this offer or neglect it at our peril?

4 God in us

Aim

To rejoice that we dwell in God and he in us.

Readings

John 17:20-26

Illustration

There is an old story about God and the humans after the Fall. Because man had separated from God through disobedience, God decided to hide from humans. He asked his angels where he should hide. 'Hide in the heights of heaven,' said the first angel. God replied, 'The humans would expect me to be in the high places and they will find me in their own high experiences.' The second angel said, 'Then why not hide in the depths?' God replied, 'Again, all human beings descend into the depths from time to time and they will discover that I am there.' One little angel had bided his time and he saw the mistakes of others. He said to God, 'Why not hide in the human heart? They will never find you there.' God smiled and said, 'How true', and from that day hid in each human heart. Yet there are so few humans who seek his presence in their lives.

5 Who is my neighbour?

Aim

To explore the question 'Who is my neighbour?'

Readings

Luke 10:25-37

Illustration

There is a story about Martin, a cobbler. He looked forward to the coming of the Lord and felt he would soon come to visit his shop. He busied himself getting ready, but he was often interrupted. He saw a child getting into trouble in the market place, so he went out to help him. Then he saw a poor woman who was in need of better shoes. He called her into the shop and saw to her needs. After this there was an old man who looked frozen. He invited the man in and gave him a warm drink. Martin would have liked to have prepared more for the coming of the Lord but he ran out of time. Martin reached out to all who came his way. That night Martin had a dream in which he saw the Lord. The Lord told him how he had visited him when the child needed help, when the woman needed shoes and when the old man wanted some warmth. In caring for his neighbour, Martin met the Lord.

6 Meeting us where we are

Aim

To know that Jesus comes to where we are and seeks to help us to rise with him.

Readings

Luke 19:1-10

Illustration

John was put in prison for the third time. He had a good mind but he used it for crime. He was a robber and occasionally given to violence. Even his family had given up on him. He rarely had any visitors other than the official prison visitors. One day he asked the man who had been coming to see him regularly why he bothered. The man explained he believed that everyone was important and could change, even John. He also told him that he was a Christian and so believed everyone was precious in the eyes of God. This really made John think: a God that actually knew him and loved him, that he need not be condemned for ever. John began to read the Gospels and the story of Jesus. He said he had never felt such a love or known forgiveness up to that time. John became a changed man. When he was released from prison he got work with an aid agency through the help of his prison visitor. He became a trusted and hard worker and in time held a position of great trust. He never hesitated to explain how he had plumbed the depths and how Jesus had reached down to him.

7 God in the here and now

Aim

To show how Jesus begins his ministry through the Church and the Scriptures.

Readings

Luke 4:14-21

Illustration

There is the story of a Celtic monk who decided to give up study and only to pray. His abbess asked how his mind would be fed if he gave up study. The monk persisted and said that he would leave where he was and go and search for God overseas. The abbess replied, 'If God cannot be found on this side of the sea, by all means let us journey overseas. But since God is near all those who call on him, we have no need to cross the sea. The kingdom of God can be reached from every land.'

There is a great need for us to know that God is with us today and God desires to bring in his kingdom through us today. Psalm 95 need always be heeded: 'O that today you would listen to his voice!' (verse 7).

8 Immersed in God

Aim

To affirm our belief in the Holy Trinity and in the mission of Christ.

Readings

Luke 3:15-17, 21, 22

Illustration

There is a species of water fly which flies in the air but dives into the water for its food. It can survive in the water because, as it dives, it takes an air bubble with it. It moves around inside the air bubble until it gets what it wants and then returns to the air. It survives in the water because it is surrounded by air.

Our God surrounds us; we are immersed in his presence. St Paul tells us this when he says 'In him we live and move and have our being' (Acts 17:28). In baptism, our being immersed in water is an outward sign of our total immersion in the presence and power of God.

9 A transforming presence

Aim

To show that the presence of Jesus transforms our lives.

Readings

John 2:1-11

Illustration

The car was running well, there was nothing wrong with the engine or the electrics but it suddenly came to a halt. It had juddered for a while and then came to a standstill. There was no way it would start again for it had run out of fuel.

The driver had to sit there on a lonely country road hoping for help. Fortunately there came a farmer on a tractor and he offered to give the car a tow. The driver was not keen as this was quite a new car. When the farmer looked he realised the car had run out of petrol. He had a full can on the farm, so he went away but soon returned and poured the petrol into the tank. He gave the petrol to the driver as a gift and said as he saw him off, 'None of us can run on an empty tank.'

There are times in life when our human resources run out. Then the harder we try, the worse it gets. There are many people who are drained or running near empty; now and again we all need our batteries recharged.

Listen to these words: 'Those who wait for the Lord shall renew their strength' (Isaiah 40:31); or these words of Jesus: 'Come to me, all you who are weary and are carrying heavy burdens, and I will give you rest' (Matthew 11:28).

10 Seek and find

Aim

To show we are all seekers and need to come to the Christ.

Readings

Matthew 2:1-12

Illustration

(This can be said by three different people.)

I bring gold because I am a rich man. I have all sorts of wonderful possessions and I have a good mind. I really am well off. I can buy whatever I want. But there are some things money cannot buy. You cannot buy love or health; you cannot buy peace of mind or eternal life. I offer gold to the One who can give me what money cannot buy.

I bring frankincense, the precious gum of a tree. Incense is used in worship. I am well-off, with a good mind. But it is easy to feel self-sufficient or over-important. I need to look beyond myself, to look at the mysteries and wonders of life. I need to know God to be satisfied. In adoration I offer incense to the One who meets my needs and tells me God is here.

I bring myrrh that relieves pain, for I have tasted many sufferings. I am a clever man but I cannot escape pain or the fear of death. I offer myrrh for all the sorrowful people of the world, for all who are heavily burdened, for all whose labour is hard. I offer myrrh for all who are in pain or distress, to the One who tells us that God cares. God will give us freedom. God will relieve our pain. God will give us life eternal.

Together:
We offer our gifts to God who gives himself to us.

11 Raising us up to God

Aim

To rejoice in the presence of the ascended Lord.

Readings

Luke 24:44-53

Illustration

A man was wandering carelessly without looking where he was going. The result was he fell into a well. The well was deep and dark, and the dirt and slime clung to the man. He knew that he could perish in this horrible place.

The God of the Old Testament, the God of the Law, came and said, 'If you had kept to the right path, you would not have ended up like this. You have strayed from the straight and narrow and now you are suffering for it. One day you will be given a rescuer.'

Allah then came and looked down at the man and said, 'It is the will of Allah. Fate has brought you here. You could not escape from this whatever you did. But it may be my will that you get out again.'

Buddha looked down on the man and said, 'Smile, for it is all in the mind. Cleanse your mind and everything will be all right.'

Jesus said nothing. He descended into the mud and mire. He experienced the dark, the pain, the discomfort. He was there in the depths taking hold of the man. Then, through great efforts that cost him dearly, Jesus rose and when he ascended he took the man with him.

12 Ready and waiting

Aim

To look at the Benedictus and to rejoice in our saving God.

Readings

Luke 1:68-79

Illustration

In the time of Jesus, when a king was about to make a journey a messenger was sent out before him. Each area would be told the king was coming. This was so that they could prepare properly. They would fill in any holes in the road and level off any awkward bumps so that the king's journey would be smooth and without hindrance.

The other task of the messenger was to make sure that people prepared themselves properly, and if the king was coming to stay, there would be room for him and that the people would give him attention.

John the Baptist was to prepare the way for Jesus, so that the people would be ready to accept him.

13 Extraordinarily ordinary

Aim

To celebrate the coming of the Saviour into the world.

Readings

Luke 2:1-14

Illustration

There was a Scottish farmer who refused to believe the Christmas story. Though his wife and children went to church, he refused to and often mocked them. Why should God lower himself to be like us? It is foolish talk.

Once when it was snowing, the family went to church. The farmer noticed that the snow was getting much worse. Suddenly he heard a thump against his window and then another. He went out to see what was happening. There in front of him was a large flock of geese which had got lost in the storm.

The farmer was kind and felt for them. He wanted to help them. He realised that they could shelter in his barn. He got behind them and tried to drive them in, but they only scattered. Then he tried by laying a trail of food to the barn door, but the geese did not take any notice. There was nothing he could do to get them to enter the barn.

About to give up on them he said to himself, 'Why don't they follow me? If I were a goose, I could lead them into the barn. If I looked like one of them, I could save them.'

Suddenly he stopped and thought about what he had said: he could only save them by becoming like them. Suddenly he understood the great love of God for humankind. He fell to his knees in the snow and gave thanks to God for his great love.

14 Jesus the Anointed One

Aim

To rejoice in the sacrificial love of Mary, which is a foretaste of the sacrifice of Christ the 'Anointed One'.

Readings

John 12:1-8

Illustration

A nurse in hospital described how humans have a great capacity for accepting what is happening to them and for enduring pain as long as they have loved ones about them and people who truly care. Pain can be borne as long as we are not left alone. We need to know in our troubles that we are still loved and cared for. Worse than pain is the feeling of separation from loved ones or a feeling that we are no longer wanted.

When many were beginning to go against Jesus – including Judas – it is good to see the expression of love and affection that is shown him from the whole household at Bethany.

15 Faith in his presence

Aim

To share in the joy of Easter.

Readings

John 20:19-31

Illustration

Archbishop Anthony Bloom was a young atheist but he was a seeker. He heard a lecture on Jesus and just could not believe what he heard. He picked up a Bible and turned to the Gospels. He counted the chapters of each Gospel so that he could read the shortest. He chose St Mark and this is what he said:

> I started to read St Mark's Gospel . . . before I reached the third chapter, I suddenly became aware that on the other side of my desk there was a presence. And the certainty was so strong that it was the Christ standing there that it has never left me. This was the real turning point. Because Christ was alive and I had been in his presence.

16 Listening

Aim

To show the need for stillness and to be receptive to our God.

Readings

Luke 10:38-42

Illustration

The greatest danger of television is that it encourages us to switch off from one another. This is true of iPods and personal CD players. They all help to shut us off and enclose us in a world of our own. But we do not need any of these to be inattentive. A child comes in with an important message but the father is filling in his tax forms and the mother is busy preparing the dinner. 'But . . .' says the child and is still not given attention. The parents have not listened and the child is left feeling alone. The generation gap is often created because we do not listen to each other. The child goes out and wonders who will look at the washing machine that is overflowing!

17 Perseverance

Aim

To show that we need to persevere in our prayers.

Readings

Luke 18:1-8

Illustration

St Teresa of Avila showed a great enthusiasm for life. In the front of her prayer book these words were written:

> Let nothing disturb thee,
> nothing affright thee,
> all things are passing,
> God never changes.
> Patient endurance
> attaineth to all things.
> Who God possesses
> in nothing is wanting.
> God alone suffices.

These are deep words indeed and should be thought about with care. (Make copies available – as a bookmark – to all who would like to think about the words.)

18 The experience of grace

Aim

To make God the centre of our prayers and to rejoice in his grace and goodness.

Readings

Luke 18:9-14

Illustration

The outside of the house looked well in the twilight. The white-washed walls seemed to shine and even more so in the moon-light. Then during the night it snowed and we awoke to a bright morning. How shabby the outside of the house looked against the brightness of the snow and the sunlight – it certainly needed a coat of paint. How we are depends on what or whom we compare ourselves with. When we are placed before the grace and holiness of God, all that we can truly say is 'God, be merciful to me, a sinner.'

19 Exploring the Lord's Prayer

Aim

To explore the Lord's Prayer.

Readings

Luke 11:1-13

Illustration

When we turn to God in prayer we acknowledge his presence: that God is with us always and that he listens to us. You are actually in the presence, in God. We are in God in the same way as fish live in water and we in air. Listen to these words by the poet Francis Thompson from the poem 'No Strange Land':

> Does the fish soar to find the ocean,
> the eagle plunge to find the air –
> that we ask of the stars in motion
> if they have rumour of thee there?

We cannot search for God but we can open ourselves to his presence, and a good way of doing this is by speaking to him quietly each day.

Use the Lord's Prayer and pause between each phrase to be aware of the fullness and wonder of the words and of your God.

20 Tuned in to God

Aim

To continue to rejoice in the Word made flesh.

Readings

John 1:1-18

Illustration

Some people live in poor reception areas for television or radio. The signal cannot get to them so the picture or the sound is blurred, fuzzy and cannot be enjoyed properly. Many things can cause bad reception. People can live too far from the transmitter. Sometimes it is just that their aerial is pointing the wrong way and it needs to be turned around. Are you sure you are pointing in the right direction? At other times it is something close that destroys reception – a motor without a suppressor, or a lot of leaves on nearby trees that can block the signal. Then again it can be the opposite: there is too much interference because the set is too receptive. All sorts of sounds distort what we need to hear. We need to be able to finely tune to make proper contact. This is as true of prayer as it is of radio waves.

21 Seeking the way

Aim

To encourage people not to 'suppose' the presence of Jesus but to seek to know he is with us.

Readings

Luke 2:41-52

Illustration

There are so many ways that people can get lost. There is a lovely story of an absent-minded professor from Edinburgh. He used to travel regularly by train and all the ticket collectors knew him. Once by the gate he was anxiously going through his pockets and after a while the ticket collector asked if he could help. 'I have lost my ticket,' said the professor. 'That's all right, sir, we all know you. You can get on the train.' 'But,' said the professor, 'I need my ticket because I do not know where I am going.'

It is easy to get lost in this world. Do you know where you are going?

22 The power and guidance of the Spirit

Aim

To know the Spirit as our strength and our guide.

Readings

Acts 2:1-21

Illustration

There are lots of ancient stories about werewolves and creatures that come in the night and steal away your life powers. You wake in the morning feeling drained and half-dead. Well, you might not believe such tales but it is still possible to awake short on energy and resources, and the more we try to put it right, the more in danger we are of becoming exhausted. When our batteries run low we need a charge from outside of ourselves. Too many of us think we are self-sufficient, able to go in our own strength, when we need to learn to wait upon the Lord for renewal and for guidance. Just as we would not drive around all day with a flat tyre, so we should make sure we begin the day filled with the power and love of God.

23 Priorities

Aim
To see where our priorities lie and how we give our time to God.

Readings
Luke 16:1-13

Illustration
Richard became a junior in the sales department of a large firm when he left school. It was soon discovered he had a flair for sales. In time he became chief salesman, and at that stage he negotiated a percentage of each sale for himself. He was becoming well-off. He had a wonderful home, two expensive cars and a good deal of shares in the business. He was made head of the sales department and then a member of the board. All was wonderful and he was rich indeed. Yet something told him all was not right. One night, returning from a sales conference, he was involved in a serious accident and nearly lost his life. Whilst unconscious he said he was aware of some being in white saying, 'Pity he has not done so well in the things that matter. This man is still a child in spiritual things.' When he recovered he went back to work for a while. His 'visitation' bothered him. He started going to church with his wife and realised he had a lot to learn and that he was poor in spirit. But he gave himself to this as he did to his work. After a year he offered himself to train for the ministry. He was ordained and after two curacies, moved to Africa with his wife and family where they worked for a relief agency. When asked about his wealth, most of which he had given away, he would reply, 'I was never as rich as I am now.'

24 Treasuring humanity

Aim

To encourage a greater sensitivity towards each other and to the poor.

Readings

Luke 16:19-31

Illustration

I know a planet where there is a certain red-faced man. He has never smelled a flower; he has never looked at a star. He has never loved anyone. He never does anything in his life but add up figures. And all day long he says over and over, just like you, 'I am busy with matters of consequence,' and that makes him swell with pride. But he is not a man; he is a mushroom!

A what?

A mushroom.

(From *The Little Prince* by Antoine de Saint-Exupéry.)
His insensitivity made the man less than human.

25 Finding true wealth

Aim

To encourage an attitude of gratitude and to make people aware of the needs of lepers.

Readings

Luke 17:11-19

Illustration

Richard was diagnosed as having a serious cancer. He had a brain tumour and if nothing was done, he would die. He was a rich and powerful man and also a man of prayer. The first thing his illness did was make him appreciate all that he had and what was precious to him. Amid the fear of what lay ahead a new joy had entered his life and his home. Each time he went for treatment he committed himself not only to the hospital team but also to the love of God. He was sure, whatever the outcome, he would not be separated from God and his care. Richard was fortunate and he was cured and given a good few years to live. He never ceased to show his appreciation for life and all that was around him. He gave thanks to God each day for all he was able to do. On top of this he gave a proportion of his income each week to Cancer Research in thanksgiving for what had been done for him.

26 Happiness in giving

Aim

To look at the relationships we have with our possessions.

Readings

Luke 12:13-21

Illustration

When John Wesley was at Oxford he lived by a rule that he set himself: 'Save what you can and give away what you can.' At first Wesley had an income of £30 a year. He then lived off £28 and gave £2 away each year. When his income rose to £60 a year he lived on £28 and gave away £32. As his income rose to £60 and then to £120 a year, he still lived on £28 and gave the rest away.

The Accountant General for Household Plate (a sort of tax collector) asked for a return from Wesley supposing he should have a good deal to show. Wesley replied, 'I have two silver teaspoons at London and two at Bristol. This is all the plate which I have at present; and will not buy any more, while so many people around me want bread.'

27 Inner peace and happiness

Aim

To show that God is our key to happiness.

Readings

Luke 6:17-26

Illustration

It is amazing how many products offer us more happiness, when in fact they are only seeking to fulfil our consuming passion to have more. The notice of 'Happy Hour' at some places is always amusing, for if that is the 'happy hour', what is the rest of the time?

There are many stories of people who have sold their heart or their soul to make money. At first it is wonderful, for money can buy all sorts of things. But possessions alone cannot fill our inner emptiness; we also need love and to know we are of some value. There is nothing worse than the person that has made it in the world but is poor in the sight of his neighbours or God. There is a very telling story from Matthew 19:16-22: the rich young man sought eternal life (did he think he could buy it?) but 'he went away grieving, for he had many possessions' (verse 22).

28 Something money can't buy

Aim

To show that Christ is our peace among the storms of life.

Readings

Luke 8:22-25

Illustration

There was a man who, for some reason, raged against life. Because he did not start off with riches, he was angry with all rich people. He did not make friends easily and often got into trouble by his aggressive attitude. Everything he gained he kept to himself. Soon he was well-off and successful – but not happy. It seemed storms followed him around. He was not comfortable to be with. He was also very lonely. Then he became ill and he began to struggle; he needed the care and attention of someone. He could afford it and hired a group of carers. One was a nurse who was willing put herself out to help him. She did errands and stayed with him for company. She also told him that she gained great peace of mind from knowing Jesus. The man was embarrassed at first but then wanted to know more. He wanted to know why she cared for him and how Jesus brought peace. In time, as his health improved, he no longer needed carers but he felt he needed this nurse; in fact, he loved her and proposed to her. She accepted him, they married and lived very happily together. He also had a living relationship with Jesus and so he knew of love and peace in his life.

29 The Midas touch

Aim

To look at the song of Mary – the Magnificat.

Readings

Luke 1:39-55

Illustration

Love matters more than riches. This is well illustrated by the story of King Midas. In his greed he accepted the offer that all he touched would turn to gold. Very exciting! He touched plates, leaves, statues and they all turned to gold. He would soon be the richest man in the world. But his food also turned to gold and he began to starve. He touched his daughter and she turned to gold and he lost her warmth and her love. He had sold himself for riches and now he was poor indeed. He had all the gold you could dream about but he was poor within. Fortunately, this condition was reversible. Midas could lose the desire for gold and become loving and happy once more. When asked if he would like this rather than gold his reply was 'Yes'.

30 The glory of the Trinity

Aim

To rejoice in the presence and power of Father, Son and Holy Spirit.

Readings

John 16:12-15

Illustration

To understand the Three in One is quite difficult. St Patrick suggested the shamrock with its three shapes that made one leaf. Clover is much the same. Others have suggested the human being as made up of body, mind and spirit: three parts that you cannot fully separate and yet one being.

You might like to think of the sun. You can see it in the sky and yet it is too bright to look at. In its glory you may like to compare the sun to God the Father. Even when the sun is hidden we know it is still there.

The sun provides the world with light. This light gives life to the world and in the light we can live and move. Let the light remind us of Jesus who is the Light of the World. Even on the dullest of days the sun still provides us with light.

The sun also provides us with warmth. Without the warmth the world would be cold and dead. In the warmth we grow and live. Let the warmth remind us of the Spirit.

Glory, light and warmth – we can talk of them as separate things and yet they are bound together. One would not exist without the other.

31 The kingship of Christ

Aim

To know that Christ is our King and wants us to share in his kingdom.

Readings

Luke 23:33-43

Illustration

In science fiction films there is often a scene when the earth or a space ship is hurtling towards disaster. No human could possible save it. Obviously they try everything they can but they just get more exhausted. Some lose hope altogether. Then a mysterious being enters the story, someone or something from beyond our world. He or she has powers beyond our wildest dreams and can change destruction and disaster into peace, calm and order. The world is restored: the being is thanked and then gone from sight.

This is a salvation story and, although fiction, understands something of our need for salvation. It knows we have no power ourselves to help ourselves. It tells of the love from a being far greater and more powerful than we are and of our salvation. There is such a story in the Gospels and it is not fiction. It is the greatest love story and rescue story of all time and yet we do not always make it our own.

32 Jesus shows God's glory

Aim

To show that in Jesus is revealed the full glory of God, for Jesus is God.

Readings

Luke 9:28-36

Illustration

On the night of 31 August 651, the young man Cuthbert was guarding sheep against robbers and wild animals. He was only 16 years old but possessed a spear and a horse. While he stayed alert and watching, the shepherds slept. The night was clear and full of stars. During the night Cuthbert suddenly saw angels descending to the earth and then ascending, taking with them a holy soul to heaven. Cuthbert sought to awaken the shepherds but they missed seeing what he saw. This made Cuthbert say, 'What wretches we are, given to sleep and sloth, so that we never see the glory of those who watch with Christ unceasingly.' The next day Cuthbert learnt that Aidan had died and he then went and offered himself to become a monk at the monastery of Melrose. True vision nearly always demands obedience and a change of direction.

33 Celebrating women in mission

Aim

To give thanks to God for our mothers and for all who have mothered us. We also give thanks to God for his loving care.

Readings

Exodus 2:1-7

Illustration

I want to tell you of a mother who had no children, yet she had a big family. Her name was Teresa and she was born in Albania. She became a nun and her work took her to one of the largest towns in the world, Calcutta. There are many people in that city and it is overcrowded. Many poor people have nowhere to go and they feed off scraps thrown out by others, often out of rubbish bins. They sleep on the streets, in doorways, under bridges. If they are ill, no one cares for them; there are not enough doctors and nurses. They have no home to go to and no mother to look after them. Teresa tried to help as many as she could and they knew her as Mother Teresa.

One day Mother Teresa saw a woman lying in the road. People were just walking past and ignoring her. Mother Teresa saw the woman was very ill. She tried to get people to help but no one wanted to know. Mother Teresa tried to get her into hospital but the doctor said there was no room for people so poorly. She went to see the health officer and he offered her two very small rooms where she could live with the woman and look after her. She did that until the woman died.

Mother Teresa got lots of women, mothers and nuns together and founded the Missionaries of Charity to care for the ill, the unwanted, for the old, for babies and for unwanted children. Mother Teresa may not have had any children of her own but many people called her Mother and she had one of the largest families on earth.

Mother Teresa often said, 'Let us do something beautiful for God', and this she did time and time again.

34 God's love is his glory

Aim

To explore how God's glory is revealed in the death and resurrection of Jesus.

Readings

John 13:31-35

Illustration

Over 150 years ago no one cared for the lepers on the Hawaiian islands. They were driven out of their homes and even off their island. The lepers were taken to a special island called Molokai. Here they were abandoned on the beach, left to suffer and to die.

One man was anxious to do what he could. He was a Catholic priest, Father Damien. He went to Molokai and was shocked at the state of the lepers. A collection of filthy ramshackle huts housed over 800 lepers. Many were helpless, weak and unable to do anything. Yet in their troubles they had built a small chapel.

Father Damien set to work. He encouraged those who were able to tidy up the mess they lived in, to build better homes and to provide a decent water supply. For 13 years he stayed with the lepers and in the end caught the disease himself. He said he was proud and privileged to be one of them. They wanted him to leave Molokai and receive better attention but he refused. Even in his last illness he gave his blankets to others in their need. He continued to show to the end his love of others, that they were not without hope and that the glory of God was for them as for others.

35 Watching and waiting

Aim

To rejoice in the light of Christ that has come into our world.

Readings

Luke 2:22-40

Illustration

As Simeon waited, his life was one of watchfulness and patience. We see a similar watchfulness in birdwatchers. They place themselves where they believe things will happen. They prepare themselves with binoculars or telescopes. Then they wait, often in silence. This is an attentive waiting, a watchful waiting; they are alert and focused on their hoped-for sighting. There was a man who went in search of a rare owl this way. He waited for three days before it appeared. He saw it only for a few moments but he said he would remember it for the rest of his life. He just had to close his eyes to see it again. He knew what it really looked like. Many of us could learn to be more attentive and watchful towards our God.

36 Glorious humility

Aim

To see that Jesus offers us a new image of power.

Readings

Philippians 2:5-11
Luke 19:28-40

Illustration

In the early twentieth century, the Mahatma Gandhi, dressed in his trademark loin-cloth, presented a curious figure – hardly the stereotypical image of an impressive, powerful leader of a nation! However, he won both the hearts and the respect of the people of India, and many others around the world to this day, who were able to see that he was offering them much more than merely a new leader. This was a radical alternative model of leadership as humble service. More than that, it was based on a way of being which sought to build relationships with others rather than dominate or control them. The devotion he inspired gave him a kind of power of which other leaders could only dream.

Jesus' entry into Jerusalem was also offering the people not merely a new king but a whole new model of kingship – and for everyone who would accept him a new way of being with ourselves, each other and the world.

37 Sight restored, life renewed

Aim

To show Jesus is the Lord of life.

Readings

Luke 7:11-17

Illustration

Pasha lived in India and his world was slowly getting darker and darker. This was hard enough to bear because his oncoming blindness meant he was losing the ability to enjoy the light of day. Even worse than this, however, was the fact that he would soon be without work due to his loss of sight. Not only Pasha but all his family would suffer. They would join the many poor and marginalised people of India. Then one day it was announced that an 'Eye Camp' was coming to his village. This was run by Sight Savers and was producing wonderful results all over India. Pasha was accepted for what was a relatively simple operation. Afterwards his eyes were bandaged for a few days and, in a sense, he felt worse off. Then came the wonderful moment when the bandages were taken off and he could see. Not only had his sight been saved but also his family had been rescued from poverty. The healing was one for the whole family and they were able to live a fuller life once more.

38 God sends and saves

Aim

To think about how God sends his messengers to us and comes himself in others.

Readings

Hebrews 13:1-8

Illustration

Sadhu Sundar Singh was the first Christian Sadhu. He suffered great persecution in his missionary travels in Tibet. Often the sadhu declared that he was rescued by angels. The following tells of such an occasion.

The sadhu was arrested for entering Tibet and preaching Christianity. The Lama condemned him to death. The sadhu was thrown into a deep dry well. The well was covered and locked. The key was kept around the Lama's waist. The remains of others who had met a similar fate were in the well. The sadhu could not see this because there was no light. For two days and nights he was without food and water. On the third day, when he was exhausted, a wonderful thing happened. He heard the key turn in the lock and the cover was removed. A rope was lowered. It had a loop in the end for the sadhu to put his foot in. He was then gently lifted to the surface. He helped his rescuer to put the cover back on the well. When the sadhu turned to thank him, he was gone. It was only some time later, when the sadhu resumed his preaching, that the Lama discovered what had happened. Yet the key was still fastened at his waist.

I am sure it was a caring human being that rescued the sadhu. Just as I am sure and agree with Sadhu Sundar Singh that it was an angel of God that set him free.

39 It's not about appearances

Aim

To know we are in the hands of God and that he can restore and renew us.

Readings

Jeremiah 18:1-11

Illustration

In the saleroom there was a violin. It looked battered and neglected. One or two people picked it up and pulled the bow across it but the sound did not seem good. The auctioneer wondered why it was in the sale. He thought it should have been scrapped. It looked a sorry sight. Most people never even noticed it. It would probably sell for a few pence.

Just before the sale an elderly gentleman came in. As the seats were filling up he went over to the violin and retuned it. Then he started to play. The music was wonderful. The capabilities of the instrument were amazing. In the master's hand, the poor-looking instrument was transformed.

When the violin was put up for auction the bidding was brisk. People realised it was a precious instrument and that it had great potential. It is amazing how things can be changed in the hands of the master.

40 Christ sets us free

Aim

To show that coming to Jesus gives us a glorious freedom.

Readings

Luke 13:10-17

Illustration

Robert was in prison for repeatedly breaking the law. He was a violent person. Taking drugs fuelled his violence. He was an addict – and that made him a prisoner as much as being in jail. He was not a likeable character and had few friends. Whilst in jail he went regularly to a rehabilitation unit to cure him of his dependence on drugs. Slowly he was freed from the habit. Whilst this was going on he had a regular visit from the prison chaplain. At first Robert rejected him and refused to listen but then he accepted a Bible. One day when he was reading St Luke the tears began to flow. When the chaplain came later Robert showed him the story of the crippled woman and said, 'Jesus has done the same for me. He has set me free.'

41 God's indestructible hope

Aim

To rejoice in the resurrection and newness of life.

Readings

Luke 20:27-38

Illustration

Have you ever been to a butterfly centre? There are a few of them around, mainly in holiday resorts, where you can see all kinds of butterflies at every stage of development. It's fascinating to see how they change from the caterpillar, crawling around the branches, through the chrysalis stage, where they could easily be thought to be dead, later emerging as beautiful butterflies soaring through the air. I often wonder whether caterpillars actually know what they will become, or whether they would find it impossible to believe until it happens.

That's the kind of transformation that resurrection life is about – something so different and amazing that we couldn't possibly imagine it until it happens.

42 Through death to life

Aim

To affirm that whatever happens our God is with us.

Readings

Luke 21:25-36

Illustration

Airports can be sad places for it is where we often say farewell to friends and loved ones who are not coming with us. We see them off and then we go to the 'departure lounge' before going to the 'terminal gate'. Don't you find those words a little threatening, if not downright depressing? You are among the departing and have come to the terminal – it sounds awful! What lifts the spirit is what is beyond. You are not stuck there, for you are off to be with a loved one, to a richer and a fuller life, or escaping from the pressures of work. The terminus is not the end but a place where we get off or set off for somewhere better.

St Luke seeks to tell us that when *things* come to an end *we* do not, for our God cares for us and is with us.

43 Love brings new life

Aim

To show that our faith is one of joy and love.

Readings

Philippians 4:4-7

Illustration

There was once a young girl who was always told off at home. Whatever she did, she was criticised (a bit like Cinderella). Nothing could please her parents and they often seemed angry with her. Never did they show their love. The girl felt ugly, she developed asthma and eczema. Later still she went into a psychiatric hospital because she was so depressed and felt useless. It seemed no one could make her better.

One day a hospital orderly noticed that beneath her sad face was a beautiful young woman. When he talked to her she was intelligent and interesting. Soon he formed a relationship with her, bringing her presents and praising the artwork she did. At this she seemed to glow. The orderly got permission to take her out on the odd Saturday. Soon they were deeply in love. Once she knew she was loved she began to smile. Her work was appreciated and soon her eczema and asthma seemed to disappear. There was a new peace and joy in her life. I can tell you she married the orderly and became a good artist. The loving presence of another had transformed her life.

44 From destruction to renewal

Aim

To enter into the joy and wonder of the resurrection and the presence of the risen Lord.

Readings

Luke 24:13-35

Illustration

High up on the moors in the winter season, men go out and set fire to the old heather. By now the heather is all twisted and gnarled; it no longer produces food for the birds and even the moorland sheep are in danger of pulling their teeth out tugging at it. The heather has become useless to the life it usually sustains. So it is burnt, but with a controlled burning. In the flames it may look as if it is totally destroyed but it is not. Under the ground its roots are safe and the men make sure the fire is not too fierce to reach the roots. In the spring the old heather is gone but little shoots appear. The heather is rising from the earth and soon will appear as fresh and as useful as ever. What was destroyed is back with newness of life.

45 Prayer-based faith

Aim

To encourage people in their use of intercessory prayer.

Readings

Luke 7:1-10

Illustration

Martin's father was a tribune in the Roman army. This meant he was a man of authority and had charge over six centurions and 600 men. When Martin was 10 years old he went to church and declared he wanted to learn the Christian faith. His pagan parents were not well pleased. The church was attractive to this young mind as the church often is to young folk. By the time he was 15 Martin was often engaged in church work. Not long after this the recruitment age for the Roman army was lowered to 16. Martin's father saw this as an opportunity and got the recruitment officer to call. He came unannounced and with manacles to take Martin off to the army. Now he would have to spend the next 25 years as a soldier. This was not a barren time for Martin. Here he would learn of discipline, obedience and orderliness. He would learn of the need to travel lightly without too many possessions, and because they were often on the move celibacy was the ideal. As the son of an officer he was soon given a commission and was allowed a servant. He shocked others by taking it in turns with his servant to clean their boots. He gave his money to the poor and cared for the needy. It was at the city gates of Amiens that Martin cut his cloak in half and gave half to a beggar.

That same night in a dream he heard Christ say to the angels in heaven, 'Look what Martin, who is still a catechumen, has given to me this day,' and showed them the cloak. Only later would Martin be baptised. Here was a Roman soldier who showed a living faith and a vital relationship with Jesus.

46 Grace is not cheap

Aim

To show that Jesus calls us to follow him and asks for our commitment.

Readings

Luke 9:51-62

Illustration

Dietrich Bonhoeffer was a German Lutheran priest who was executed by the Nazis for his resistance to their evils. He says this concerning the cost of discipleship:

> Cheap grace is the deadly enemy of the Church . . . cheap grace is the preaching of forgiveness without requiring repentance, baptism without church discipline, communion without confession, absolution without contrition. Cheap grace is grace without discipleship, grace without the cross, grace without Jesus Christ, living and incarnate.

47 The mission of the seventy

Aim

To explore the mission of the seventy.

Readings

Luke 10:1-11, 16-20

Illustration

Picture coming home on a dark night. All the lights are out in the whole area. There must have been a power cut. Everyone is in the dark. The only glimmer of light comes from the church. You are a bit nervous and you go in. There is someone sitting in the sanctuary and he is surrounded by light. You sneak forward and see that he has nail marks in his hands and feet. You know it is the Christ but his feet are fastened by chains and his hands are tied. The Christ is unable to move. You come close and ask, 'Lord, your feet are fastened and your hands tied – why?' The Christ replies, 'My feet are fastened and my hands tied because my people do not pray regularly. They do not reach out to others in love. They do not share in my saving works. I have entrusted my work to them and they have not accepted the light I have offered them. Things will only change when you share with me: when you see Christ in others and be Christ to others.' Suddenly you are aware of this truth, and lights start coming on all over the place.

48 Dedication and practice

Aim

To show we need to be active in our faith and that we need to practise.

Readings

Hebrews 11:29–12:2

Illustration

There were two brothers. Both were runners. One was very good and won most races when he was small. He always used to beat his brother. Because he could run well, he decided he did not need to train. It was more fun playing computer games and going out with his friends. He thought practising was a waste of time. The other brother knew that he had to improve his style. He practised often. He practised sprinting and long-distance running. He did exercises to increase his breathing powers and his physical ability. He was seen on the track most nights. His brother said he was wasting his time. By the time they were in their teens, the brother who had been the best now lagged far behind. He was paying the price for not practising and keeping his eyes on what he could do. His brother was now winning competitions and all sorts of prizes. If asked how he became a better runner, he said, 'By a lot of practice and by being willing to dedicate myself to the job.'

49 The Communion of Saints

Aim

To rejoice in the communion of saints.

Readings

Luke 6:20-31

Illustration

A man presented himself to the minister leading the service once it was over. 'I would like to become a Christian.' The minister enquired what had brought him to this decision. Was it a sermon, a book or some event in his life? The man was a little embarrassed at this point and said how he read little and hardly ever attended church. 'It's my boss at work – he is a real tough chap and we are a hard bunch of men – it's the way he deals with us. I wanted to know what made him so sensitive and caring, what made him strive to be honest and fair to all. He told me it was because he was a Christian. If that is what a Christian is like, that is what I want to be.'

The best advertisement for God and for our faith is the way we live and witness to what we believe.

50 Faith on a cheerless day

Aim

To show that, though troubles will come, our God is with us.

Readings

Luke 21:5-19

Illustration

Life was often bleak for the people who lived in the Hebrides. Sometimes the future did not seem to hold any promise and when the mists came down it did not help. Here is an affirmation prayer that faces the reality of the cheerless day but also a much deeper reality of the love of God and our future in him.

> Though the dawn breaks cheerless on this isle today,
> my spirit walks in a path of light.
> For I know my greatness.
> Thou hast built me a throne within thy heart.
> I dwell safely within the circle of thy care.
> I cannot for a moment fall out of thine everlasting arms.
> I am on my way to thy glory.
>
> *Alistair Maclean, Hebridean Altars*

51 Temptation is everywhere

Aim

To encourage people to face temptation with faith.

Readings

Luke 4:1-13

Illustration

Anyone who is still alive is tempted, so do not say you are not tempted. If you are not tempted, you have never lived or you have let something in you die. There is always a tug of war between good and evil, between achieving and failing to do so. There is no place or person free from this battle. In the book *Rogue Herries*, Hugh Walpole tells of how Herries had come to the wild and lonely Lakeland where he met a travelling preacher called Robert Finch. Herries asked:

> 'How shall I like this place? It is cut off from the world.'
>
> There was a sudden odd note of scorn in the little man's voice as he answered, 'It is the world, sir. Here within these hills, in this space of ground is all the world. I thought that while I was with my Lord Petersham that the world was there, but in every village I have passed since then I have found the complete world – all anger and vanity and covetousness and lust, yes, and all charity, goodness and sweetness of soul. But most of all, here in this valley I have found the whole world. Lives are lived completely . . .The mountains close us in. You will find everything here, sir. God and the devil both walk in these fields.'
>
> *Rogue Herries*, Part 1, by Hugh Walpole

52 Trusting God's promise

Aim

To show how God can be trusted to keep his promises.

Readings

Genesis 15:1-12, 17, 18

Illustration

In a dream a man was told where there was treasure hidden in a nearby castle under a blue stone. The dream was quite clear and he could remember every bit of it. Yet he did not bother even to see if the stone was there in the castle. He told his dream to a friend. His friend went immediately and found a great treasure under the blue stone. He became very rich and although he was generous toward his friend, his friend realised that because he had not bothered when an opportunity was offered him he had missed out in a big way.

How often do we miss out on the fullness of life because we do not take up the promises of our God?

53 A life of purpose

Aim

To show how our lives have purpose and are meant to be useful.

Readings

Luke 13:1-9

Illustration

Abraham Lincoln triumphed over many adversities to become the President of the United States. Here are some of his words and they are about all of life and not just gardens:

> Die when I may, I want it said of me that I plucked a weed and planted a flower wherever I thought a flower would grow.

Think of the purpose of our existence as expressed by The Shorter Catechism of 1647:

> What is the chief end of man?
> To enjoy God and to glorify him for ever.

54 Living to God's glory

Aim

To show that if we are faithful in small things, then we will be trusted to do greater things.

Readings

Luke 5:1-11

Illustration

Denzil was always talking of giving glory to God. The house he lived in was a tip. Every room was untidy if not unclean. Denzil continued to talk of praising God but gave little respect to the people around him. He seemed unaware of his surroundings or of others, only full of himself. One night he heard God in his dreams saying, 'If you want to serve me, start where you live. Give glory to me by tidying up your part of the world. You will hear me better if you learn to listen to others.' Denzil awoke, aware of how ugly his room looked. That day he started to clean up and get rid of rubbish. Soon he redecorated the room and added fresh curtains. He scrubbed himself and got new clothes. He seemed to be a different person: he actually glowed. If someone needed a person to listen or to care, Denzil was the one. By being attentive to small things, God had called him to do greater things for him.

55 Freedom in giving and receiving

Aim

To show that Jesus wants us to have the glorious freedom of the children of God.

Readings

Luke 6:27-38

Illustration

In the Holy Land there are two seas, the Sea of Galilee and the Dead Sea. The same river, the Jordan, feeds both of these seas. The Sea of Galilee teems with life: there are fish in its waters, trees grow near its shoreline, birds visit it and their singing can be heard. The Dead Sea lives up to its name: it does not sustain life, it is too salty to allow plants to thrive and the birds do not like its saltiness. One sea has life and the other is dead, yet the same river feeds both. What is the difference? The answer is quite simple: the river Jordan flows into one end of the Sea of Galilee and out of the other. As the Sea of Galilee receives, so it gives out. The Dead Sea does not have an outlet. All the water that flows into the Dead Sea is kept; it does not give out. The sun evaporates the water and the salts are left behind. Because the Dead Sea does not have an outlet, it dies. By keeping all that it receives, it chokes itself of life. Sadly there are people just like that.

Hearing the Shepherd's voice

Aim

To explore our relationship with Jesus through the image of the shepherd.

Readings

John 10:22-30

Illustration

Two flocks of sheep had become intermingled. Night was coming down and it would be very difficult to separate them before it was dark. If men or dogs were sent in, it would cause a lot of fear among the sheep and greater confusion. The shepherd who came to care for his flock said, 'Leave them alone. Wait until it is almost the end of day, then I will call mine. They know me, they will hear my voice and follow me.' As evening came, the shepherd started to call. The reaction among the sheep was interesting, for some heard the voice and wanted to run away because they did not know it. The sheep that belonged to the shepherd recognised his voice. They heard a call that meant safety, shelter and sustenance. They knew of the love of the shepherd and came running to where he was.

57 Deepening our relationship with God

Aim

To seek to deepen our relationship with God.

Readings

Luke 17:5-10

Illustration

George Matheson looked forward to a good life. He was studying for the ministry. He was preparing to marry the one he loved. Then he began to go blind. His world began to go into darkness. He lost many of his friends, and his loved one decided she could not cope with a blind man and left him. His world was shaken but not his relationship with God. George Matheson wrote the hymn 'O Love that will not let me go'. The second verse is 'O Light that follow'st all my way' and the third 'O joy that seekest me through pain'. George had faith in a great God. The final verse 'O Cross that liftest up my head' affirms not only his steadfast relationship but God's relationship with him. Now *that* is faith.

58 God's gift of peace

Aim

To show that Christ is the Prince of Peace.

Readings

Luke 8:26-39

Illustration

We cannot create peace but we can accept it. Peace is a gift from God to us. We can accept it by living in a peaceful way. The mind can often be in turmoil like a raging sea and yet God is there and offering us his peace. Peace is not an absence of activity but rather a working in harmony with the world around us. Peace comes through a right relationship between others and us, but, above all, between God and us. Peace is God's gift and will help us to get back in tune with everything, but if we persist in staying out of tune with others or the world it is hard for God's peace to get to work in us.

59 Proclaiming the story

Aim

To see Jesus as the risen Lord on the shore of Galilee.

Readings

John 21:1-19

Illustration

It is told that when Jesus returned to heaven, the Archangel Michael barred his way. The archangel said, 'How can you return to heaven? Your work is not yet completed. There are many who do not know about or who have not heard of your saving acts.' Jesus said, 'I have left my friends to complete what I have begun.' The Archangel was amazed. 'Do you mean those puny, often straying humans?' 'Yes,' said Jesus, 'I trust them and I know that through following me they will bring my gospel to all the world.'

60 Humbly open to God

Aim

To encourage people to make contact with Jesus.

Readings

Luke 7:36–8:3

Illustration

Someone was described as 'a self-made man worshipping his own creator'. Think about this for a moment. Often what keeps a person from God is the illusion of self-sufficiency. Some say they have grown up and do not need such a Father figure. Yet none of us will survive without God. The strange thing is the closer someone comes to God, the more aware they are of their own weakness and sin. St Paul spoke of sinners and said, '. . . of whom I am the chief'. St Francis said, 'There is nowhere a more wretched sinner than I.' God can deal with those who are aware of their sins. He can reach out to them in forgiveness. He can reveal his love in accepting the sinner. The self-righteous and the self-sufficient set up their own barriers and are far harder to approach. Those who come to God aware of their sin and weakness are the ones who discover his power in their lives and his love.

Topical index

Numbers refer to Illustrations and not to pagination.

Bible reference index

Numbers refer to Illustrations and not to pagination.

Acknowledgements

The Publishers wish to thank all those who have given their permission to reproduce the following copyright material.

Page 30
The following extract from *The Little Prince* by Antoine de Saint-Exupéry:

> I know a planet where there is a certain red-faced man. He has never smelled a flower; he has never looked at a star. He has never loved anyone. He never does anything in his life but add up figures. And all day long he says over and over, just like you, 'I am busy with matters of consequence' and that makes him swell with pride. But he is not a man; he is a mushroom!
>
> A what?
>
> A mushroom.

Page 52
The following extract by Dietrich Bonhoeffer:

> Cheap grace is the deadly enemy of the Church . . . cheap grace is the preaching of forgiveness without requiring repentance, baptism without church discipline, communion without confession, absolution without contrition. Cheap grace is grace without discipleship, grace without the cross, grace without Jesus Christ, living and incarnate.

Page 56

> Though the dawn break cheerless on this isle today,
> my spirit walks in a path of light.
> For I know my greatness.
> Thou hast built me a throne within thy heart.
> I dwell safely within the circle of thy care.
> I cannot for a moment fall out of thine everlasting arms.
> I am on my way to thy glory.

Hebridean Altars, Alistair Maclean, Hodder & Stoughton.

Every effort has been made to trace the owners of copyright material and we hope that no copyright has been infringed. Pardon is sought and apology made if the contrary be the case, and a correction will be made in any reprint of this book.